HOMOSEXUALITY AND EDUCATION

To the memory of my parents;

for David (though he does not want it);

and for Marcus.

By education most have been misled;
So they believe, because they so were bred.
The priest continues what the nurse began,
And thus the child imposes on the man.

JOHN DRYDEN

HOMOSEXUALITY

AND

EDUCATION

J. Martin Stafford

MANCHESTER

1988

Published by the author at the
Students' Union Building,
Oxford Road, MANCHESTER, M13 9PR.

 British Library Cataloguing in Publication Data

STAFFORD, J. Martin (John Martin), 1948–
Homosexuality and Education.
1. Homosexuality. For teaching.
I. Title.
306.7'66'024372

ISBN   0 9512594 1 5

Printed in Great Britain by
Antony Rowe Ltd., Chippenham.

Preface

The treatment of homosexuality within the school curriculum has become an extremely controversial issue in the last couple of years since two or three local education authorities resolved to deal with the subject positively. Even where such a policy has been promoted with moderation and sensitivity, it has attracted vituperative criticism from the radical right and from some of those who call themselves Christians. While I was in the midst of writing this book, it has become seriously threatened by legislation specifically enacted to curb the 'promotion' of homosexuality and to prohibit the presentation of any homosexual cohabitation as a 'pretended family relationship' or the suggestion that it is 'acceptable'.

As sexual orientation appears to be determined at an early age by unknown factors, Clause 28[*] of the 1988 Local Government Act, supposing as it does that homosexuality can be promoted, is proposterous. However, inasmuch as this legislation constitutes — among other things — an unprecedented interference with open enquiry and free speech within the state education system, it is extremely sinister and should be resisted by all who resent such unwarrantable infringement of liberty. It is also strikingly inconsistent with the kind of libertarianism to which the Conservative Government usually pays conspicuous lip service. It must now seem

[*]originally numbered 27 and briefly renumbered 29.

ironic that in June, 1984, Margaret Thatcher, along with the heads of six other industrialised countries, signed a declaration of democratic values, which stated:

> We believe in a rule of law which respects and protects without fear or favour the rights and liberties of every citizen, and provides the setting in which the human spirit can develop in freedom and diversity.

But then it is not unusual for politicians to mouth lofty sentiments to which they do not genuinely subscribe. Indeed, duplicity and hypocrisy are arguably the very stuff of which political life is made.

Although I cannot claim to be entirely non—partisan, I have aimed to examine the issues with which this work deals more fairly than has been done hitherto. It is not addressed to those who espouse a set of moral prejudices speciously riveted into cohesion by a system of religious beliefs and who refuse to recognise that Judaeo—Christian prohibitions against homosexuality were formulated long before there was adequate understanding of the phenomenon they condemn; for no arguments would ever prevail upon such people. It is rather directed to those who are willing to examine the facts dispassionately and to adopt practical solutions which will relieve the needless hardships which many now suffer.

I have endeavoured to present my views as straightforwardly as possible. Chapter 2, however, incorporates in summary form all the work I have done on sexuality and the foundations of ethics since the early 1970's when the issues first seriously preoccupied me as a postgraduate student. This chapter is therefore — inevitably — both highly technical and more concise than the importance of its subject—matter should allow. A more complete exposition of my views may be found in the four articles to which I have referred. I have used

vi

material (sometimes reproduced verbatim) from three of them, and am grateful to the editors of the journals for permission to do this.   These are:

'On distinguishing between Love and Lust' *Journal of Value Inquiry* Vol. XI No. 4 (1977) pp.292–303.

'Hume, Spencer and the Standard of Morals' *Philosophy* Vol. 58 No. 223 (1983) pp.39–55.

'Love and Lust Revisited: Intentionality, Homosexuality and Moral Education' *Journal of Applied Philosophy* Vol. 5 No. 1 (1988) pp.89–102.

I have also used in Chapters 1 and 5 material from my article 'In Defence of Gay Lessons' *Journal of Moral Education* Vol. 17 No. 1 (1988) pp.11–20.   Again, I thank the editor for permission to reuse this.

I am pleased to acknowledge my indebtedness to the following people: to Dr. John Harris of Manchester University, who urged me to write this work; to Professor Peter Campbell of Reading University, who brought relevant material to my notice and made detailed suggestions after reading early drafts of chapters; to Allan Horsfall, who supplied me with press cuttings and read drafts of some chapters; and to Harry Lesser and Gavin Fairbairn for their encouraging and constructive comments.   The opinions expressed are, of course, my own and I am solely responsible for any errors which remain.

March, 1988.

Contents:

1. Is Homosexuality Natural?

Because so much of the criticism directed against homosexuality depends on the allegation that it is unnatural, this issue is an appropriate point at which to begin. In his *Treatise of Human Nature*, the philosopher David Hume (1711–1776) outlines some possible senses of *natural*, and concludes that anything which is either not miraculous, or not the result of human artifice, or not rare or unusual can justifiably be called natural.[1] Since homosexuality satisfies all three of these conditions, its claim to be regarded as natural is particularly strong. Nevertheless, the tendency to view it as unnatural seems in our own culture to have been almost irresistible. The Finnish philosopher and sociologist Edward Westermarck (1862–1939) must be accounted among the most cool and dispassionate of inquirers; yet even he begins his account of the phenomenon by describing it as falling "outside the ordinary pale of nature". However, only two sentences later and without realising his inconsistency, he declares, in concert with other scientific research, that "it is frequently met with among the lower animals [and]...probably occurs...among every race of mankind."[2] Accordingly, the contention that homosexuality is unnatural is palpably false.

Even so, it is only in the last 120 years that the homosexual has been recognised as a distinct kind of person. The term *homosexuality* was not coined until 1869, and did not become current in English until the

1

1890's. [3]   In earlier times, "homosexuality was regarded not as a particular attribute of a certain type of person but as a potential in all sinful creatures". [4]   It was not until the mid—nineteenth century that the congenital nature of the disposition was acknowledged. This development was resisted by the censorious and moralistic, as it implied a diminution in the responsibility of those who behaved homosexually and made the maintenance of legal sanctions seem less appropriate. However, the transition was from a criminal to a medical explanation, and brought no immediate alleviation to the lot of homosexuals; for homosexuality was seen not as an innocuous variant but as an indication of evolutionary regression or even innate moral degeneracy.   A pre—revolutionary Russian sexologist, Veniamin Tarnovsky, while conceding that homosexuals could not help themselves, ascribed their condition to damage in their parents' genes occasioned by "hysteria, epilepsy, alcoholism, anaemia, typhus, debauchery, soil, climate or altitude". [5]   Even as late as 1965, an opinion poll reported that 93% of respondents saw homosexuality as an illness requiring treatment.   One needs little imagination to appreciate why the medical model of homosexuality instilled several generations of homosexuals with a profound sense of inferiority and inadequacy.

The strategy of questioning whether homosexuality is inherent or rather a perverse mode of behaviour freely chosen by the godless and depraved is once more increasingly deployed by those who are keen to represent homosexuality in the worst possible light.   By reviving an old controversy and, as it were, re—enacting a scene from the history of ideas, they tacitly acknowledge that the recognition of the involuntary nature of homosexuality was a development conducive to more humane treatment and latterly to wider social acceptance, and therefore one that is inimical to their retrogressive aspirations.   Dr. Adrian Rogers grudgingly concedes that it is "possible although far from certain that some individuals are created homosexual by birth" and that "such unfortunate

2

individuals should be met with tolerance and compassion but not with encouragement". His belief that homosexuality can be spread by the campaigning activities of Gay Rights groups and by social attitudes which are too accommodating prompts him to claim that "many have been converted who might otherwise have had normal and socially useful sex—lives". [6] However, he adduces no evidence whatsoever in support of his thesis, the counterfactual nature of which necessarily renders it unverifiable.

The fact that more homosexuals are now openly so does not constitute a proof that homosexuality is more widespread. In any case, Roger's argument does presuppose that homosexuality is intrinsically undesirable. While it is true that "if practised by a majority of citizens it would eventually destroy society because it embodies a sterile childless relationship with no future generations", such a possibility is extremely remote. As long as its incidence did not increase to the point where it threatened demographic stability, his argument would have no cogency. Moreover, nowhere in his pamphlet does he criticise those heterosexuals, be they married or celibate, who choose — sometimes for entirely selfish reasons — not to have children. The reader may well be amazed that Dr. Rogers, an influential voice in the Conservative Family Campaign, should measure the usefulness of people's sex lives solely by their progenitive capacity. Now there are many feckless and irresponsible persons who, having neither enough money nor enough sense to supply their own needs — let alone those of children, breed almost as prolificly as rabbits, constantly spawning more like themselves to the great detriment of the communities they live in and of the nation as a whole. Does Dr. Rogers really regard their sex—lives as socially useful, or is he merely being disingenuous in pretending to do so? Conversely, there are others who are homosexual or celibate whose social utility would, on more orthodox criteria, be indisputable.

Rachel Tingle, who has devoted herself to vehement campaigning against homosexual equality in the sphere of education, refuses to accept that growing up to be homosexual is a process as spontaneous and natural as growing up to be heterosexual. She says, with undisguised incredulity:

A universal theme within the gay movement is the idea that homosexuals are not responsible for the way they are but, rather, while growing up they simply 'discover' that they are homosexual. Becoming homosexual is thus seen as a process of maturity rather than anything involving conscious choices on the part of the individual. [7]

I am at a loss to know why Tingle should find this so hard to believe. She presumably has no difficulty in accepting that most people grow up to discover that they are heterosexual, so why cannot she accept that a significant minority do grow up realising that they are homosexual? No one knows *why* they do; but *that* they do is not disputed by anyone who examines the evidence with an open mind. Given the large numbers of people who declare themselves to be homosexual, her scepticism with regard to the spontaneity of their desires has no obvious justification. It is, for example, less warrantable than that of the King of Siam who, on being told by the Dutch Ambassador that in Holland during winter the water sometimes becomes so hard that it could bear the weight of an elephant, promptly accused the ambassador of lying. [8] Tingle's stance amounts, in effect, to contending that because she and most other people are heterosexual, then everyone must be. In fact, research shows very plainly that most homosexuals recognise their sexual feelings by their early teens. In a survey of thirty—six gay teenagers, [9] twelve to fourteen seems to be the age at which most of them knew for certain that they were homosexual. Many report an awareness of embryonic sexuality at a much earlier age. Thus their sexual awakening comes no later than that of

4

heterosexuals and is usually identified despite all the cultural norms which favour repression. Moreover, if, as Tingle maintains, being homosexual were a matter of choice, why does she think anyone would choose to be a member of a group which is widely regarded with hostility and so unjustly discriminated against? In this, as in other respects, people do not have a power to determine their own constitution. This point was well expressed early in the eighteenth century by Francis Hutcheson, whose remarks, though not specifically intended to refer to sexual orientation, are entirely applicable to it.

> ...Our Perceptions of Pleasure or Pain do not depend directly on our Will. Objects do not please us, according as we incline they should. The Presence of some Objects necessarily pleases us, and the Presence of others as necessarily displeases us. Nor can we, by our Will, any otherwise procure Pleasure, or avoid Pain, than by procuring the former kind of Objects, and avoiding the latter. By the very Frame of our Nature the one is made the Occasion of Delight, and the other of Dissatisfaction. [10]

The thesis expressed by Hutcheson's observation is endorsed by Professor Antony Flew in the passage quoted on page 8 below, where he says that homosexuality is no more alterable at will than is heterosexuality — and for the same reasons. Accordingly — but again contrary to what Tingle would like to believe — homosexuality, like heterosexuality, is indeed an integral part of one's personality, which is why people who are homosexual do not usually want to change, unless they are subjected to coercive pressure of an improper kind.

When she says that the involuntary nature of homosexuality is a universal theme within the gay movement this is not strictly true; for some gay activists and radical feminists have embraced a doctrine which is

5

the inversion of her own and is equally silly. It claims that heterosexuality is the result of conditioning and propaganda, the redressing of which would liberate people and enable them to choose their own sexual orientation.[11]   These fanciful and deluded theorists have mistaken effects for causes: for that literature, advertising, and social institutions are predominantly heterosexist *reflects* the fact that most people are heterosexual, but is not the *cause* of this.   The contention that heterosexuality is largely the result of conditioning is inconsistent with our certain knowledge that sexual propagation was around long before sexual propaganda was even thought of, so the former cannot be the effect of the latter.   Most animals are heterosexual, but it would be fatuous to suppose that their concupiscent inclinations were induced by exposing them to 'heterosexist propaganda'.   Moreover, if sexuality *were* the result of conditioning, then since our own society is pervaded by 'heterosexist propaganda', one would expect homosexuality to be very rare indeed, or even to have been completely eradicated by two thousand years of Judaeo—Christian censure.

Although the myth that homosexuality is a sickness is now almost entirely discredited, it is one which Tingle tries to perpetuate.   It seems to be like the hydra: each time you lop off one of its ugly heads, it sprouts another; for similarly crude attempts to draw wide—ranging conclusions from limited and unrepresentative data were avidly cited by David Holbrook in 1972[12] and by Mary Whitehouse in 1977.[13]   Referring to a single work, Tingle contends that homosexuality is an illness attributable to severe disturbances in the early child—parent relationship when critical maturational changes are taking place.[14]   This and all similar arguments can be countered with devastating force by a very general observation made in 1944 by the late Professor C.D. Broad.

Of all branches of empirical psychology that

6

which is concerned with what goes on in the minds of babies must, from the nature of the case, be one of the most precarious. Babies, whilst they remain such, cannot tell us what their experiences are; and all statements made by grown persons about their own infantile experiences on the basis of ostensible memory are certainly inadequate and probably distorted. The whole of this part of psychology therefore is, and will always remain, a mere mass of speculations about infantile mental processes, put forward to explain certain features in the lives of grown persons and incapable in principle of any independent check or verification. Such speculations are of the weakest kind known to science. [15]

Tingle then proceeds to complain that when the American Psychiatric Association voted to delete homosexuality from the official list of pathologies, it did so under pressure from gay activists rather than as a result of scientific research. Now the pertinent question is surely whether there was ever any scientific warrant for its inclusion in the first place, or whether, as seems far more likely, the facile presumption that homosexuality is an illness was made in all too eager compliance with the prejudice in which Judaeo—Christian culture is steeped. Moreover, it is not unduly cynical to suppose that the American psychiatrists would never willingly have abandoned so lucrative a doctrine had they been able to put forward a remotely plausible defence on its behalf; for they probably raked in more over the years by retailing 'cures' for homosexuality than the Vatican every amassed from selling indulgences. In fact, it is possible to categorise a condition like homosexuality as a mental illness only by extending the concept of mental illness in such a way as to render it unserviceably contentious or even viciously ideological. Those who are pleased thus to castigate homosexuality would therefore do well to remember that in the U.S.S.R. it is Christians and other anti—Soviet dissidents who help to fill the mental hospitals.

One of the most witty comments on the thesis which equates homosexuality with mental illness was made by Professor Antony Flew in 1971:

> ...the whole point of talking of any sort of health or disease — as opposed, perhaps, to appealing to moral or other non—medical ideas or norms — must be to press a supposed analogy with the paradigm of physical health or physical disease.
> Now in a typical case of physical disease: there is first something organically wrong...; then, second, the symptoms are not under the immediate present control of the patient...; and, third, the patient himself complains (and what he complains of is the disease itself, and not just the disease considered as the cause of whatever social penalties may happen to be imposed on those who have it).
> A moment's thought shows that not one of these requirements is generally met by practising homosexuals... First, they could not be practising if the apparatus were not in good working order. Second, though homosexuality as a character trait is no more alterable at will — and for the same reason — than is heterosexuality, there is, surely, no reason to believe that the homosexual is any less, or any more, able than the heterosexual to inhibit the expression of his disposition in what — in the old pre—four—letter days — movie publicists used to call 'acts of love'. And, third, though some homosexuals may be disgusted with their homosexuality — just as many of the Christian saints were disgusted with their heterosexuality — many others would have no complaints about their condition were it not for the penalties which are still imposed on them by society. [16]

To classify otherwise ordinary people as ill simply because they are disposed to love someone of their own sex is as perverse as it was to punish children who were left—handed. It is as if someone who had seen only trees whose branches grow upwards concluded that a weeping willow tree must be unhealthy simply because its branches droop, and resolved to cut it down. [17]

As for religious arguments, many of those who appeal to the scriptures to sustain their condemnation of homosexuality do so only because its words accord with their own prejudices. At the same time, they are content to practise or at least to condone flagrant worldliness, greed, and other behaviour which conflicts no less violently with the injunctions of the religion which they outwardly profess. But in any case, no objection founded on religious belief can be more secure than the religion on which it is based. That most of the corpus of Christian theology is hotly disputed, even among those who call themselves Christians, and is also either unsupported by or inconsistent with our empirical knowledge should greatly diminish the force of all arguments rooted therein. In recent decades, the validity of traditional interpretations of scripture has been challenged by theologians [18], and more liberal and enlightened Christians now readily concede that comprehensive biblical prohibitions against homosexuality are difficult to reconcile with our knowledge of human nature and therefore ought not to be regarded as binding. Moreover, since believers are a minority of the population, their convictions in such a matter, impinging as they may well do on the liberties of others, have little claim to be regarded with sympathy.

In 1986 the Catholic Church made a desperate attempt to dig in its doctrinal heels on this point by issuing a *Letter to the Bishops...on the Pastoral Care of Homosexual Persons.* On sexuality as in other matters, its attitude to science is decidedly ambivalent. In a pronouncement which is tantamount to "heads I win: tails you lose", it declares: "the Church is...in a position to learn from scientific discovery, but also to transcend the horizons of science and to be confident that her more global vision does greater justice to the reality of the human person..."[19]   Thus in the twentieth century, as in times past, the Catholic Church will invoke or contradict the findings of science according as its interests require. The document states unequivocally that all homosexual activity is 'an intrinsic moral evil' and the disposition to it 'an objective disorder'. Any contrary statements made by the 'pro—homosexual movement' are dismissed as 'deceitful propaganda'.[20] Thus the Holy See not only thinks fit to reaffirm the full rigour of its traditional obdurate dogma, but also does not scruple to impugn the good faith of all who dissent. Now surely, an institution which has in its time, and to suit its convenience, burned heretics, sold indulgences, condoned the persecution of Jews and the systematic pillaging of South America, and to this day discountenances the use of contraceptives even in countries where people are starving to death — surely, I say, such an institution cannot expect to command unquestioning allegiance as an arbiter of morals. Of course, all the usual passages from *Leviticus, Romans,* and *Corinthians*[21] are paraded before us; and yet the authors conveniently overlook the fact that homosexuality is a phenomenon which pervades the whole of the animal creation, not one which is confined to postlapsian man. Perhaps, after all, the intentions of the Creator are more reliably manifest in His works than in the writings of those who lay claim to His inspiration.

If this recent pronouncement were everywhere dismissed with the contempt which it deserves, it would give less cause for concern; but many look to the church for guidance and some, no doubt, act upon the directives which it issues. The Catholic Church is in the paradoxical and morally odious position of being willing to accommodate as lapses from grace transient and promiscuous homosexual encounters, whilst at the same time it condemns loving and committed relationships deliberately entered into and conscientiously maintained. An American bishop admitted as much during a television interview.[22]   But the most cynical feature of

10

the *Pastoral Letter* is surely the mealy—mouthed passage which pretends to deplore the malice which is sometimes directed towards homosexuals, but then goes on to assert that if they are so brazen as to press for social acceptance or civil rights, violent reaction is what they must expect.[23] Was there not a time when some people said similar things about Catholics? Indeed, are there not places where they still do? In the face of such provocation I feel justified in echoing the harsh words used by James Beattie to counter Malebranche's repudiation of Aristotle: Fie, Cardinal Ratzinger! Popery, with all its absurdities, requires not from its adherents so illiberal a declaration![24]

2. Is Homosexuality Wrong?

As we have just seen, the Catholic Church maintains that homosexual activity is an intrinsic moral evil: Rogers and Clements contend that it is 'fundamentally wrong'.[1] When people make statements of this sort, they appear to be attributing a certain property, namely 'moral evil' or 'fundamental wrongness', to a particular kind of action — in this case homosexual activity. Before we can begin to assess whether these assertions are justifiable, we need to consider more precisely what they mean — and even whether in fact they mean anything precisely. Since the rise of logical positivism in the 1920's there have been some philosophers who believe that a sentence such as "Homosexuality is fundamentally wrong" is not factual or even quasi—factual as are other possible sentences of the same form, e.g. "Hydrogen is inflammable." Being inflammable is a natural property, which can be tested for by non—controversial scientific procedures (e.g. holding a naked light close to a substance will show how inflammable it is). That there are no corresponding ways of determining the moral nature of an action has prompted some thinkers to conclude that sentences which evince the speaker's moral sentiments are more akin, logcally, to those such as "This roast beef is very tasty"; that is, they merely express the attitude of the speaker. On this view, when Rogers and Clements say that homosexuality is fundamentally wrong, their utterance amounts to nothing more than an imposing and pretentious way of telling their readers that they hate homosexuality.

The classic rejoinder to such a subjectivist analysis of moral language is that such utterances are not merely expressions of personal feeling but do indeed express genuinely objective judgements. Moral good and evil, it might be urged, are non−natural properties which can be intuited by all, or at least by certain people, provided they attend with sufficient care to the situations they wish to appraise. The controversy as to whether there are non−natural moral qualities has been alive in one form or another since early in the eighteenth century, when the first plausible naturalistic moral theories were propounded. Non−naturalistic theories are ontologically very uneconomical, postulating as they do an extra−sensory realm of other−wordly properties and entities. It is true that one cannot *prove* that there are no such things (just as one cannot disprove the existence of ghosts and fairies), but they are to my mind a needless encumbrance serving only to obfuscate and mystify moral issues. However, if one denies the existence of any ontologically independent 'moral reality' one must either gravitate towards moral nihilism or propose an alternative theory which can explain the non−arbitrariness of morality.

It is the latter course which I propose to pursue. The question as to how we distinguish good from evil was current throughout the eighteenth century. Some historians of ideas have suggested that the issue had been brought to life much earlier than this by the disunity of Christendom caused by the Reformation and the consequent lack of a universally recognised moral authority. However, there were two more immediate circumstances which prompted the investigations of the writers whom I most admire: first was the spirit of enquiry which stirred them to examine moral and social questions in the same experiential way as Newton had approached the natural sciences; second was the publication of Bernard Mandeville's *The Fable of the*

Bees (1714, second edition 1723), which maintained (in a manner precursory of Gay Liberation Front ideologues in our own time[2]) that morality was solely a product of human artifice whereby politicians had made selfish men more tractable by implanting in them the notions of honour and shame. Francis Hutcheson (1694—1746) strove to establish that virtue was natural to mankind without the mediation of such political artifice. In opposition to Mandeville he claimed both that man was basically benevolent rather than selfish, and that he was endowed with a God—given and unanalysable moral sense which determined him to approve of certain actions and characters (namely benevolent ones) and to disapprove of their contraries. He did not postulate a moral reality independent of this capacity to feel approval and disapproval, the orientation of which he ascribed solely to God's own benevolence. Because God is benevolent and wished to promote the happiness of his creatures he endowed mankind with a moral sense concordant with his own benevolent intentions. However, He could conceivably have given us 'a contrary determination of mind' and made us approve of malevolence, but that would have been inconsistent with His benevolent purposes.

Hutcheson's intellectual successor was David Hume, whose ethical theory was akin to Hutcheson's in that he too made morality relative to human nature and did not believe in any kind of extra—sensory moral reality[3], but unlike Hutcheson he undertook to account for the operations of our moral sentiments by analysing and explaining their psychological components. In their attempts to explain how we distinguish moral good from evil, both of them supposed that human nature was uniform; that despite appearances to the contrary there was an underlying unanimity about good and evil, and that this constituted the criterion of morality. Unfortunately, the unanimity which they postulated, and sometimes defended by the most convoluted arguments, is largely illusory. Accordingly, while their theories were

14

— in Hume's own words — "a considerable advancement of the speculative sciences"[4] in that they recognised that moral distinctions are dependent on the sensibilities of human beings, they failed to provide a satisfactory criterion of moral rectitude.

Though it has been unfashionable for most of this century to say so, I think that such a criterion is suggested by the direction of evolutionary development — a phenomenon of which eighteeth century writers were, of course, unaware. Although hesitant intimations of the possibility of social evolution recur in Hume's writings, they conflict with and are contradicted by his more pervasive assumption that human nature is uniform.[5] The diversity of moral response which mankind undoubtedly displays constitutes an important weakness in theories of moral sense or moral sentiment such as those of Hutcheson and Hume. For if human nature fails to exhibit the kind of uniformity which they thought can provide a standard for moral judgement, where is that standard to be sought? Where there is real and deep—rooted conflict of moral sentiment, how — if at all — can it be resolved? The writings of Herbert Spencer go some way towards solving this problem.

In *The Data of Ethics* of 1879, Spencer considers the evolution of conduct and character under three aspects: as it affects (i) self—preservation; (ii) the rearing of offspring; and thence (iii) the maintenance of the race, observing that advances in these kinds of conduct are interdependent. Living as he did in an age of rapid progress and unbridled optimism, he envisaged an as yet unrealised state of affairs where all conduct would be perfectly evolved — that is to say, where all creatures would be so perfectly adjusted to their environment that the ends pursued by each would be consistent with the well—being of all the others. He also hinted at the development from mere peaceful co—existence to universal co—operation. Why, in Spencer's view, is such active co—operation necessary, and under what conditions is its development possible?

As man becomes more advanced, his requirements become increasingly multifarious — so much so that each individual could not possibly aspire to provide them all for himself. The more advanced his state of development, the more heterogeneous must be the co−operation which takes place; that is to say, a larger number of people must collaborate; they must have different functions, and thus make diverse contributions to the corporate effort. This social process is in fact a particular instance of Spencer's general law of evolution, namely that it is "...a change from an incoherent homogeneity to a coherent heterogeneity..."[6] Advances in civilization and co−operation take place concomitantly: the latter making possible the former, the former making necessary the latter.

Obviously, co−operation can take place only in social units where internal aggression has been largely eliminated and trust established. Accordingly, civilized societies will tend to be characterised by those norms and sentiments which are conducive to internal harmony and inter−personal confidence. Practices which operate directly against such stability will always be severely censured, while those whose ill−effects are more remote and therefore less evident may be tolerated. Thus while murder, larceny and untruthfulness are invariably proscribed among civilized people as being wholly incompatible with a highly organised social life, various forms of intemperance and unchastity may be regarded with more indulgence, since the harm which they immediately occasion accrues primarily to the participants, while the social ill−effects are more remote: "...the social consciousness, not distinctly awakened to the social results, does not always generate consistent social sentiments."[7]

Now certain characteristics of human nature and certain standards of conduct (e.g. honesty, contractual

16

and sexual fidelity) do undoubtedly seem to have been favoured by the evolutionary process, and to have been so favoured inasmuch as they are conducive to the co−operation which advances civilization and as they are predictive of that further development which Spencer envisaged. The evolutionary process, therefore, has tended to vindicate these standards as pragmatic. Accordingly, the theory of evolution not only explains the diversity of morals, by postulating different stages of moral and social development, but also suggests how we might adjudicate between conflicting moral sentiments. For according to Spencer's doctrine those moral sentiments should be counted privileged which empirical evidence suggests are favourable to the co−operation necessary in a civilized society, or which could be deductively shown to be requisite for such further developments as he thought to be highly probable. [8]

What are the implications of all this for sexual morality? Quite simply that certain capacities, attitudes, and ways of behaving have the endorsement of evolution and others not. I shall now proceed to argue that the distinctions between love and lust and the conduct to which they respectively give rise are of the utmost moral importance. What do we mean when we say that someone entertains feelings of love or acts in a loving way, as opposed to that he entertains feelings of lust or acts in a lustful way? It is not difficult to prove that there are different phenomena to which the words *love* and *lust* should be discriminatingly assigned. These phenomena can conveniently be subsumed under two main heads: *viz.* the behavioural (i.e. conduct openly manifested) and the phenomenological (i.e. states of consciousness known directly to each of us only through introspection).

Since conduct, unlike states of mind, is susceptible to public observation, I shall begin by considering the modes of behaviour which, even in the estimation of the less thoughtful, tend to distinguish love from lust.

Firstly, casual associations of a very transitory kind would not usually be called loving, save in the weakest sense of the word. We should surely look askance on someone who declared that within a very short time he had indulged in a series of intimate associations with a large number of people with whom he was not previously acquainted nor likely ever to see again, and yet that he loved them all. We should be sorely tempted to ask whether he knew what love was, pointing out that such sentiments as are more usually denoted by that word cannot arise and decline within so short a duration, nor be directed towards so many different people either concomitantly or in such rapid succession. We should conclude that he was using the word *love* in a weak, not to say degenerate, sense. Our scepticism would be due not only to the discordance of his language with ordinary usage, but also to our realisation that his claims were inconsistent with our knowledge of human nature. For love, in contradistinction to lust, usually includes a desire to have a prolonged relationship with another person and also a concern to promote his or her long—term welfare.

As there are certain types of conduct which distinguish love from lust, so there are certain states of mind to which these modes of conduct are postively correlated. Of the former the following instances will suffice: with someone we love we are inclined to spend our time, to do for him such things as will please, and to manifest our affection by those agreeable familiarities which it is unnecessary to expound upon here. Of the states of mind characteristic of love I list the following: the contentment which the presence of a loved one brings; the uneasiness or distress occasioned by his absence; satisfaction at his propserity; anxiety at the prospect of his suffering any harm. Obviously, neither of the above lists is exhaustive. I submit, then, that relationships of the kind which are commonly called loving in a strong sense are distinguished from those which are merely lustful by the behavioural and phenomenological characteristics outlined above.

So far I have claimed only that love and lust are distinguishable by differences of conduct and feeling. I shall now proceed to argue that love is characterised also by a difference in the level of conceptual awareness of its object; that objects of love must be *intentional objects* whereas the objects of lust need only be *material*. Intentional objects are those objects of thought which are *con*ceived rather than merely *per*ceived. Thus the chair that I sit on, the painting I look at and the person I see are — in the first instance at least — *material* objects; whereas the chair that I remember, the painting I imagine, and the person whom I love are *intentional* objects. They may also exist materially, but they need not do so; for my memory of the chair may not be veridical, and both the painting and the person I love may be no more than figments of my imagination. That objects of love must be intentional while objects of lust need not be is borne out by the following consideration. It is impossible to love a person without having an integral (albeit possibly erroneous) conception of him; whereas lust can be aroused merely by the prospect of certain physical features. Were this not so, pictorial pornography would be as unmarketable as spent matches. The claim that intentionality is one of the features distinguishing love from lust was first made by me more than a decade ago. [9]

The crucial point is that all the features outlined above — behavioural, affective and cognitive — which distinguish love from lust are equally applicable to homosexuality and heterosexuality. Even Roger Scruton, who would dearly like to believe that homosexual desire is morally inferior to heterosexual desire, has conceded that both are capable of the same interpersonal intentionality and that therefore homosexuality is not intrisically obscene or perverted. [10] To revert to the moral assessment of sexuality, what is important is the distinction between love and lust as constituted by the features outlined above; whether it be homosexual or heterosexual is irrelevant. This judgement is supported by the application of the evolutionary ethical criteria earlier advanced; firstly because love, requiring as it does the high degree of cognitive activity necessary to make its objects intentional, is confined to the most highly evolved species, namely man; and secondly because, as Herbert Spencer observed a century ago, the fruits of unbridled lust are inimical to civilization and social progress.

Firstly, the nurture of offspring is more effectively achieved where a stable monogamous relationship guarantees the supportive presence of the father. No welfare state, be it ever so bountiful, can supply this factor where it is wanting. On this issue my views accord substantially with those of Rogers and Clements, who point out that "fatherless families are more likely to produce ignorant children who reject authority and are led towards delinquent behaviour"[11] and that children of one—parent families grieve for the departed parent, have poor self—images, and are more likely to be emotionally disturbed.[12] The prevalence of unchastity tends therefore to the production of inferior individuals and consequent social decay. Secondly, promiscuity[13] undermines rather than promotes "those higher sentiments... — affection, admiration, sympathy — which in so marvellous a manner [have] grown out of the sexual instinct"[14], thus severing the higher from the lower components of the sexual relation and rendering inactive what would otherwise be a powerful incentive to stable relationships of the socially requisite kind. Thirdly, since social altruism grows out of family altruism, promiscuity, entailing as it does an unwillingness to subordinate personal gratification to the welfare of others, is inimical to social cohesion. Since the first argument is relevant only to heterosexuality, it is by no means apparent why Rogers and Clements should regard homosexuality as intrinsically threatening to family life; for homosexual households can surely co—exist quite

20

happily alongside ordinary families. However, the other two apply to homosexual and heterosexual relationships alike and constitute a cogent reason why civilized societies discountenance promiscuity.

This chapter began by considering pronouncements that all homosexual relationships are morally wrong. I have argued that since they are susceptible of the same qualitative variations as heterosexual relationships, they should be appraised by the same criteria according as they are stable, responsible and loving or promiscuous, wanton, and exploitative. The indiscriminate censure of homosexuality meted out by the Catholic Church and other conservative moralists would now command little support, were it not for the adverse publicity about AIDS, much of which has been irresponsibly generated by the tabloid press. Unfortunately, as Spencer wrote in 1861, "the suppression of every error is commonly followed by a temporary ascendency of the contrary one."[15] In accordance with this maxim, the last two decades have witnessed a reaction whose excesses have proved more pernicious than the features of traditional morality which provoked them. Gay activists have almost invariably allied themselves with those who have sought to remove sex from the moral realm altogether, maintaining that the private conduct of consenting parties is not a matter of legitimate social interest, provided they avoid unwanted pregnancies and the transmission of venereal diseases. Notoriously, but predictably, these evils have *not* been avoided, and the same siren voices which once lured people towards them and denounced public concern about private misconduct are now loud in demanding public funds to relieve its adverse consequences.

The arch—enemy of human happiness and social stability is not homosexuality but promiscuity. Even if it brought no material ill—effects in its wake, it would be commended only by those who take a very superficial view of sexuality — a view which disregards both the emotional richness of which human relationships are capable and the poverty of those which are loveless. The ideal of interpersonal relationships based on a reciprocal intentional awareness is espoused by Roger Scruton[16] as well as by myself. It is also, I believe, endorsed by the process of evolution. In contrast, promiscuous and impersonal sexual activity should be discountenanced not just because of its dire material and social consequences (considerably aggravated as they are since the advent of AIDS), nor even because it falls short of the ideal, but because when persisted in it disqualifies its participants from ever attaining that ideal or even from aspiring to it. It is not mere prurience or prudishness which gives sexuality so prominent a place among our moral concerns. It is the contingent but indisputable fact that this is an area in which homosexuals and heterosexuals alike have an enormous capacity both to confer and receive benefits and to inflict and suffer harm.

3. The Legacy of Liberationism.

In this chapter I shall chronicle some of the aberrations of the homophile movement during the 1970's. It is not my contention that only harmful things were done in this period. On the contrary, much useful work was accomplished: the establishment of social groups, of supportive services for people who are distressed or in need of advice; legitimate campaigning to bring about law reform in Scotland and Northern Ireland as well as to redress anomalies remaining in England and Wales and to secure equal treatment for homosexuals in employment and other areas. However, while such activities did not gain much media coverage and never hit the headlines, more negative and sensational happenings were widely reported at the time, continue to be recalled by those who are hostile to the cause, and have helped to bring about the marked polarisation which now bedevils issues which concern homosexuality — and none more so than its treatment within the school curriculum.

The politicisation of homosexuality on party lines is a comparatively recent development, and dates from 1970. Before the 1967 Sexual Offences Act, supporters and opponents of law reform were to be found in the ranks of both major political parties, though the readiness to support reform was much greater in the Labour and Liberal parties than among the Conservatives. It was Mr. Humphrey Berkeley, the Conservative member for Lancaster, who introduced a reform bill during the

1964—6 Labour government, but a Labour member, Mr. Leo Abse (Pontypool), who later sponsored Lord Arran's Bill as it progressed through the Commons to the Statute Books. The two Sir Cyrils (Black of Wimbledon and Osborne of Louth — both Conservative) were no more vehement in their opposition than the Mahon brothers Peter and Simon, Labour M.P.'s for Preston South and Bootle respectively.

It was not until the arrival of the Gay Liberation Front in the autumn of 1970 that the supposedly revolutionary nature of homosexuality was proclaimed. This doctrine was founded upon the conviction that "the taboo against homosexuality was so deeply embodied in Western civilization...that only a revolutionary overthrow of its structures could truly liberate the homosexual". [1] Accordingly, any compromise with bourgeois society was out of the question. In an account of the excesses of the GLF written with the benefit of hindsight by a former supporter, Simon Watney too declares that the early ideology of the GLF equated sexual liberation with the destruction of capitalism and the demise of the family. [2] Along with this went an inversion of all 'bourgeois' values. However, the inverted values were no less categorical than those they were meant to displace. Communes were established which forbade pair—bonding (the then current sociological jargon for stable monogamous relationships) and denounced the impulse towards it as the result of bourgeois conditioning. [3] Other features of GLF dogma were the need to identify with all 'oppressed' groups (e.g. women, blacks) and a determination to regard their shared oppression as resulting from a single cause, namely a deliberate conspiracy on the part of the ruling class. There is no more evidence of any such premeditated and on—going conspiracy than there is of a 'social contract' made in the remoteness of antiquity, and the 'oppressions' of which GLF complained (now commonly called sexism, racism, and heterosexism) manifestly stem from widely disparate economic, political and religious causes.

In general, the ideology of GLF was a ragbag of incoherence and contradiction: in particular, it is ironical that while endorsing promiscuity the movement pretended to deplore the objectification of sexual partners. Presumably its adherents believed in the possibility of deep and meaningful one night stands. Moreover, the much—vaunted liberating potential of Marxist analysis has never been realised under the sway of any Marxist government. It did precious little for those homosexuals who were unceremoniously dragged through the streets of Havana in the aftermath of Castro's 1959 Cuban revolution, nor has it borne fruit in the Soviet Union, where to this day homosexual practices remain illegal. It ought to have been obvious to the ideologues of GLF that since prohibitions against homosexuality predate the rise of capitalism by more than two millenia, it cannot be in capitalism that they are primarily rooted (for no effect can anticipate its cause). They must rather be rooted in features of the more pervasive Judaeo—Christian tradition.

It was not only that the theories of GLF were unsound: its policies were palpably impracticable and its structure (if it could be said to have had one) incohesive; moreover, it was always without a clearly specified programme of action. Perhaps its supporters hoped that the bastions of capitalism would crumble before their rhetoric as did the walls of Jericho when Joshua commanded his trumpeters to play. Accordingly, GLF had waned to insignificance within two years of its inception. However, its spectre has continued to haunt us, and still lends a tenuous credibility to the claim that homosexuality is subversive. For to this day its manifesto is cited by those who wish to discredit even moderate proposals conducive to homosexual equality, and when they speak of 'homosexual ideology' it is that of the GLF which they mean, although it was never espoused by more than a vociferous minority, who were more committed to revolutionary politics than to the welfare of homosexuals. [4]

The plausibility of the homophile movement was damaged throughout the 1970's by its own injudicious actions. From its inauguration in the late 1950's the Homosexual Law Reform Society had always boasted an impressive array of honorary vice — presidents (including archbishops, bishops, peers, lawyers, doctors and professors), whose patronage brought considerable prestige and respectability to the cause. In the autumn of 1971 the Campaign for Homosexual Equality, of which I was the Treasurer, resolved to extend the list of its own patrons, who until then had been confined to about ten clerics, academics and other high — ranking professionals. Among the people whose support was to be solicited were Mick Jagger, Kenneth Tynan, and Richard Neville. At this time Mick Jagger was involved in allegations of drug — taking, Kenneth Tynan was the promoter of the show *Oh! Calcutta*, which I believe was the first to bring the spectacle of gratuitous full — frontal nudity to the London stage, and Richard Neville was facing the prospect of imprisonment for publishing *The School Kids Oz*. It was resolved that if any two members of the Executive Committee opposed any name, then that person should not be invited to become a vice — president. Of the twelve EC members, I was alone in declaring that these three persons would add no lustre to our organisation, and so my opposition was ineffective. I therefore called a meeting of existing vice — presidents to try to secure their intervention. The EC, resenting my attempts to thwart its democratic decision, subsequently resolved to remove me from office as Treasurer and demanded my resignation as an EC member. I refused to resign, but submitted myself for re — election (and was duly re — elected) in February, 1972. My being deposed as Treasurer of CHE was an event of no great importance and was not widely reported[5]; but the circumstances which led to it were indicative of the prevailing spirit of the time and an ominous portent of things to come.

At its 1975 conference in Sheffield, CHE (from

which I had resigned completely in July, 1973) showed its solidarity with a group of paedophiles, whom it was still fashionable to regard as yet another 'oppressed minority'[6]. The harm thus perpetrated was considerable. *Homosexual* and *paedophile* are by no means coextensive terms: very few homosexuals are paedophiles and most paedophiles are heterosexual. Since homosexuals are widely but wrongly perceived as a threat to the young, it was surely an act of egregious folly for an organisation purporting to represent their interests to be seen rubbing shoulders with one whose professed aim was to legitimise the molestation of children. This incident provoked immediate denunciation from a *Guardian* columnist, John Torode, who exclaimed "Thus far and no farther": he for one was going to climb off the trendy liberal bus. [7] In a subsequent issue Peter Hain, an honorary vice−president of "the once highly respectable CHE", expressed the strongest reservations: "Some plain speaking is called for: paedophilia is not a condition to be given a nod and a wink as a healthy fringe activity in society − it is a wholly undesirable abnormality..."[8]

A long−running and more widely reported saga was the prosecution in 1977 of *Gay News* and of its editor Denis Lemon for publishing a poem describing homosexual acts between Christ and his disciples and the sexual violation of his body after the crucifixion. The offending work was subsequently deemed to be a blasphemous libel and the presiding judge, imposing on Lemon a fine of five hundred pounds and on *Gay News* one of a thousand pounds, described it as 'appalling' and 'scurrilously profane'. [9] The prosecution had been brought privately by Mrs Mary Whitehouse, whose action enjoyed considerable support, including that of many homosexuals, who no doubt felt indignant at the disgrace which the action of *Gay News* had brought upon them. A publication which had never been slow to bewail the insensitivity with which homosexuals are often treated had shown itself all too willing to ride rough−shod over the feelings of Christians and those who, though not committed, none the less respect the deity and institutions of that religion.

In the 1980's much harm has been inflicted by the publicity surrounding AIDS — a sexually transmitted disease which is rightly associated with promiscuity and loose — living of the kind which many homosexual 'spokespersons' were once only too happy to condone, although not all who have contracted this horrible disease are guilty of such faults. There is an understandable reluctance on the part of homosexual organisations to admit as much[10], but, when all is said and done, if AIDS were a disease which, like influenza or mumps, came adventitiously upon its hapless victims rather than one which is spread through a dissolute and abandoned lifestyle, it would be *pro rata* no more serious a problem in New York and San Francisco than it is in Limerick and Inverness. Accordingly, the unsavoury images of homosexuality which AIDS has helped to promote have militated against its acceptance as potentially a responsible and legitimate way of living. To cite but one particularly flagrant instance, on January 26th 1987, the BBC 1 Programme *Panorama* included a report from San Francisco in which one man admitted that prior to the AIDS epidemic there had been places to which homosexual men might resort and in the course of a single weekend have as many as *fifty* different sexual partners. Such revelations surely make those much — maligned inhabitants of Sodom seem like paradigms of chastity and restraint, and serve to evoke in people of ordinary sensitivities the most intense and well — founded feelings of disgust.

Outlined above are some of the ways in which the gay movement, by its own irresponsible conduct, has fortified the prejudices of those who are unsympathetic and alienated others who were once well — disposed. They represent a sorry object lesson in how not to win friends and influence people; for such actions have done more to bring discredit to the cause of homosexual equality than all the ranting fulminations from a host of homophobic preachers could ever have achieved. They have helped to sustain a climate in whch bigotry can be given a specious justification and exploited for political ends. Since 1985 the process of polarisation has been furthered by the adoption at Labour Party Conferences of motions supportive of homosexual rights and the pursuit of concordant policies by councils under Labour control. All such measures, irrespective of their merits, are now condemned as a matter of course by unprincipled Conservative politicians, who have been quick to learn that invective against homosexuals is certain to find favour with many voters and also accords well with a catch−cry taken up in recent years by their own party, namely the sanctity of family life and the propriety of Victorian values − a phrase whose ambiguity must be particularly welcome to a party which in the last five years has had a chairman who consorted adulterously with his secretary, a deputy chairman who gave two thousand pounds to a harlot (albeit not for services rendered), and a vice−chairman cited as co−respondent in the divorce proceedings of the man whom she subsequently married. Despite these facts, its unseemly posturings of unimpeachable respectability continue unabashed and unabated.

During the run−up to the 1987 General Election the Conservatives conducted a well−staged campaign of vilifiction against those London boroughs which are trying to eradicate prejudice by positive and constructive treatment of homosexuality in schools. In December 1987, the Government adopted in the Local Government Bill a clause originally proposed by a private member and designed − among other things − to outlaw in maintained schools the presentation of any homosexual cohabitation as a 'pretended family relationship' or the suggestion that it is 'acceptable'. Clearly, the aim of this legislation is to inhibit *any* positive and non−censorious discussion of homosexuality. While some of its principal advocates may have been fired by truly

Christian zeal, the measure was supported by nearly all Conservative M.P.'s, many of whom were no doubt activated by more dishonourable motives; for, realising that the sympathetic policies of some councils have alienated many of Labour's traditional supporters, they are eager to exploit this by jumping onto the bandwaggon of popular prejudice. Homophobic Christians and politicians alike would do well to reflect that those who fall victim to the bigotry which they have set out to nurture may well be their own children or grandchildren, since homosexuality — unlike bad housing or poor diet — is not confined to any one social class but is quite random in its incidence. The polarisation and politicisation of this issue, unjustified as it is, has none the less become an insuperable obstacle to any consensual approach in education, even though young homosexuals whose parents are of all political persuasions suffer similar adverse effects. The nature and extent of these problems I shall now proceed to consider.

4. Where Ignorance isn't Bliss.

Homosexuals — and in particular young homosexuals — encounter many problems as a result of ignorance and the hostility which it engenders. I shall illustrate these by referring to the experiences of people whom I have interviewed personally, to cases which have been documented elsewhere, to a fictitious account whose elements are sufficiently authentic to be worthy of attention, and to the figures made known to me by organisations to whom young gay people turn for help. I shall begin by alluding to David Rees's short novel *The Milkman's on his Way*. One reason for my choosing this book (apart from its suitability to my purpose) is to defend it against the unwarranted castigations of Rachel Tingle, who evidently regards it with particular animosity. I should not have expected her to read it sympathetically, but I think that she should have studied it with greater care and described it more accurately. So basic a duty she owed both to the author whose work she was criticising and to the people who would read her own. For a scrupulous regard to the principles of fair dealing is one of the marks which distinguish honest scholarship from deceitful polemic.

As Tingle says, this book does indeed relate the sexual awakening of a Cornish teenager, Ewan Macrae, whose first experiences are with a heterosexual friend; but to call them 'sexual experiments'[1] makes poor Ewan (who on my reading comes over as a good—natured and innocuous boy) sound like Frankenstein or a clinical

31

vivisectionist. Moreover, Tingle's phrase is particularly inappropriate given that the instigator of these incidents is the heterosexual friend, Leslie. Ewan later has a week—long "holiday romance" with a London teacher. No matter how many attempts she makes (and I have counted four)[2], Tingle always mis—states the age of at least one member of the pair: Paul is 23, not 21, and Ewan is 17 (17¼ to be precise), not 16 as Tingle usually claims. She does not mention that the ending of this relationship leaves Ewan feeling heart—broken, but makes great play of their age—difference (which in a heterosexual or a lesbian relationship would be of no account), of its criminal implications, and of her false allegation that they engage in anal intercourse on the beach.[3] Only one sexual encounter is specifically stated as taking place on the beach, and it is not an act of anal intercourse. When David Rees is describing venery, he leaves little to be supplied by his readers' imagination (a circumstance which, I readily admit, renders his work less than ideally suitable for use in schools); so it is difficult to excuse Tingle's mistake in this particular. I raise these issues merely to set the record straight before I examine the features of Rees's novel which are relevant to my present concern.

The first half of the book renders a poignant account of Ewan's problems, some or all of which are shared by most young homosexuals. Moreover, many of them are peculiar to homosexuals, who have in addition to cope with the strains and stresses common to all young people. The first issue raised is that of the concealment and pretence which are forced upon young gay people as they awaken to their own sexuality in a world which treats it as alien. The pressures are twofold: first, to conceal their real feelings and inclinations; second, to pretend to inauthentic ones.

Dad read the *Sun* every day, mostly the sports section. He took it with him on his round, and sometimes I would find him ogling the girl on page

three. 'A right little cracker,' he said on one
occasion. 'Isn't she?' I had a good look: it was
expected. As was my agreeing with his assessment.
But she did nothing for me; she was just so much
bare flesh. A girl with extremely large tits. So
what? I felt uneasy. It was bad enough, living a
life of pretence with Lousie, Leslie and the others;
but I had learned to cope with that. Now it
seemed to be intruding into other areas of my
existence: would I be able to get by? I'd be found
out. That was my worst fear... On subsequent
mornings, I was often asked for my views on the
girl of the day. 'I wouldn't turn *her* down,' was
his comment on one of these creatures, who was
sticking her bottom out in a supposedly provocative
manner. I thought she looked quite revolting. [4]

Later in the book Ewan reflects bitterly:

A gay existence meant lie after lie would have to
be told, particularly to my parents. The gulf
between me and them suddenly seemed a vast
chasm, I'd have to be two people, one for home,
one for away. It was tragic. Hateful and wicked.
I began to feel as I had when I first realised —
there was something loathsome about me. [5]

The dishonesty which is imposed on homosexuals
can easily lead to self—loathing as well as to a sense of
alienation. Ewan, like any decent and good—natured
young person, longs to be open and communicative with
his parents, [6] but his fear of their reaction to his
declaring that he is homosexual inhibits him from raising
the issue. Some young homosexuals do find the courage
to 'come out' to their parents, but the decision is almost
invariably taken after much agonising and acted upon
with great apprehension and foreboding — and with good
reason; for some parents reject their homosexual
offspring[7]; others react with incredulity or patronisingly
suggest that it is only a passing phase; while few are

whole—heartedly accepting and supportive — at least not initially. Young heterosexuals are not subjected to any comparable strain, as Ewan reflects when comparing his own state of alienation with that of his friend Leslie, who could easily tell his mother that he had met a nice girl and expect her to be warmly received into the house.

> God! How it hurt just looking at Leslie and hearing him mention — almost as a triviality — those enviable things which were forbidden to me. It hurt! *It hurt!!* Parents not minding you having a loving, stable relationship. Letting you bring your girl—friend back home, including her in the events and routines of the family. And if you got married, presents to help furnish a house. Hold hands anywhere. Kiss in the streets. Book a double room in a hotel and no eyebrows raised. But me? Others like me? [8]

Other problems which are depicted are his loneliness and depression, particularly after the ending of the week—long romance with the London teacher, Paul.

> But it certainly hurt. As much as the fact that he wasn't there any longer. The days were an aching, yawning, lonely emptiness. The weather broke, and there was no more surfing. And no jobs, anywhere. I spent a lot of time writing in my diary. I'd been duped: it had been just another bloody holiday romance. September. October, November. I felt almost suicidal at times. Then just before Christmas, I experienced another shattering blow. [9]

The diary in which he had kept an account of his experiences is found by his mother and read by both parents, whose reaction, while not violent, is extremely unfavourable. To my mind this event underscores the desirability of coming out to parents if this is at all possible rather than allowing them to make the discovery for themselves. If young people decide to come out, then the time and circumstances are of their choosing. They can prepare for it, and the very fact that they are making the move gives them the upper hand psychologically. Conversely, when, as in Ewan's case, parents find out and the young person is not prepared, he is at once put on the defensive. What Ewan's parents say to him would be deeply hurtful to most youngsters. At the time, Ewan has been feeling intensely lonely and depressed and is therefore particularly vulnerable. His mother vacilates between incredulity and self—reproach.

> 'It's not your fault', my father said. 'It's not mine either'. I was about to say that it wasn't anyone's fault; I was like that and probably always had been. Maybe from birth. But he added, 'There's always one rotten apple in any barrel.' The shock of those words was like having a bucket of cold water thrown in my face.[10]

Not long afterwards his mother bursts into tears again and tells Ewan:

> 'I wish you'd never been born! Oh God! I wish I was dead.' My father moved to her, protectively. He looked at me and said, 'See what you've done?'[11]

This incident shows that it is not only homosexual offspring who are adversely affected by the negative attitudes of those around them. Ewan's parents suffer almost as much as Ewan, since they feel needlessly alienated from their only child. The familial relationship is blighted not by Ewan's homosexuality but by his parents' prejudiced attitude towards it. Had they been better informed, they might well have been able to accept it unreservedly, thus sparing themselves and their son much unhappiness. Although *The Milkman's on his Way* is a work of fiction, I have cited it because it presents a vivid account of experiences which are only too real to many gay teenagers. Two books which record factual instances of isolation, despair, alienation, abuse and other problems are *Breaking the Silence — Gay Teenagers Speak for themselves*[12] and *Something to tell you*[13].

The pressures upon homosexuals to appear heterosexual or even to try to make themselves *become* heterosexual seem to operate more forcefully on young lesbians than on young gay men. This may be because they are more likely to receive overt advances from members of the opposite sex than their male counterparts. Of the sample in the London Gay Teenage Group survey, more than three fifths of the women (61%) had had their first sexual experience with someone of the opposite sex compared with only a quarter of the men[14]. Those who espouse the view that heterosexual activity might provide a 'cure' for homosexuality are disposed to welcome the social pressures which favour conformity, but the evidence is that such pressures force people into relationships for which they are ill—suited, often to the suffering and detriment of both parties if the relationships are ultimately terminated with animosity and recrimination.

I turn now to consider problems centred on school rather than the family. In its issue of 12th June, 1987 *Capital Gay* reported a case involving particularly vicious abuse of a 16—year—old fifth former in a north London comprehensive school. In a series of incidents, he suffered insults and threats, was hit over the head with a bicycle chain from which he sustained cuts and bruises, was spat at, had his books thrown at him and a bookcase pushed over on top of him, and was sexually assaulted by a gang who then punched and kicked him. All this took place when he was studying for 'O' levels. In the autumn of 1987 I myself interviewed two fifteen—year—olds who had suffered verbal abuse not only from pupils but — what is far more deplorable —

36

from teaching staff. One had been told that he and another boy were walking along 'like a couple of queers', and the other had been called a faggot by a P.E. teacher in the presence of other boys. Although he had not declared his homosexuality to classmates, he was suspected of being gay and was the object of an increasing amount of verbal abuse and ridicule. This is hardly suprising if teachers are seen to entertain anti—homosexual prejudice and to encourage it by their own example. His life at school was becoming increasingly miserable, and his worries were compounded by his fears of the effect that this would have as he approached the GCSE exams.

Although many young homosexuals do well in school and go on to further and higher education (as is witnessed by the existence of gay societies in most universities and polytechnics), Catherine Hall has suggested that the performance of those who are less gifted or who come from less stable backgrounds may be further depressed by the adverse forces which confront them because they are homosexual. Writing of her work with a gay youth group, she says:

> When I began talking to individuals about their experiences it became apparent that schools had failed miserably to identify problems or to support youngsters crying out for help... For those already disadvantaged by social deprivation, insecurity about their sexuality is yet another problem to be overcome before they can make the most of their education. [15]

Her survey of 34 young gay men disclosed that their problems escalate rapidly as they go through secondary school, where feelings of isolation, depression, and confusion militate against concentration and lead to a marked falling off of academic achievement. After leaving school they generally felt frustrated and bitter about their school experience.

Needless to say, gay pupils cannot be certain of a sympathetic reception or competent advice if they avail themselves of the pastoral guidance which schools are now expected to provide. In the most recent edition of *School's Out*, Andrew Stark records an instance of a fifth former with a firmly developed gay identity who approached his head of house during a time of domestic crisis. The head of house broke his trust by reporting their conversation to the boy's parents (who, fortunately, already knew that he was gay) and gave him a lecture about the age of consent, which he (the head of house) mistakenly believed was 18. The boy received no real support whatsoever, and since he naturally felt disinclined to vouchsafe further confidences to the housemaster, his only means of access to the school's pastoral system was effectively blocked.[16] One wonders how many teachers have pastoral responsibilities which ignorance and prejudice disqualify them from discharging to good effect.

To whom might gay youngsters have recourse if they feel they need help? The Samaritans do not keep records classified according to the nature of their clients' problems. However, a letter to the *Times Educational Supplement* of 6th November 1987, prompted by an ill—informed contribution from a Yorkshire vicar[17], claimed: "The tragedy of the gay son of the homophobic family is all too familiar to Samaritans." The Manchester Gay Switchboard receives around 16,000 calls per year, of which approximately 20% are from people under 21, and half of these (i.e. about 1,600) are from people under 17. These figures, which probably represent only the tip of a much larger iceberg, are indicative of much needless unhappiness. Such services are generally confined to larger towns and cities, so young homosexuals who grow up in smaller towns or rural areas are even more likely to experience intense isolation.

An organisation exclusively devoted to helping gay teenagers and their parents is Parents' Enquiry. It was founded in the late 1960's by Rose Robertson after she had come to accept her own son's homosexuality and realised that the distressing experiences of his adolescent years were not peculiar to him. It is now sustained by her and a dozen helpers. She sees two or three people almost every day — over 800 a year. 75% of those who call upon her assistance are between the ages of 14 and 17. The predominant age range used to be 16 to 18. She attributes this reduction to a general lowering in the age of sexual awareness. An alarming 30.8% have attempted suicide, and she has encountered at least one case of actual suicide in each of the last ten years. Those who consult her complain of isolation, but by far their greatest fear is of adverse parental reaction to their being homosexual.

In the present polarised political climate it cannot be emphasised too strongly that homosexuality is evenly distributed among all social groups. Since it appears to be entirely random in its incidence, it is just as likely to affect the children of barristers as those of binmen. In the survey of over 400 conducted for the London Gay Teenage Group, 180 respondents described themselves as working class, while 192 accounted themselves middle class.[18] Rose Robertson has also remarked on the great diversity of her early experience before founding her movement.

We had single parent families where a boy had been brought up by his mother; single parent families where the child had rarely seen his mother; single children, and children from large and average families; children from caring, secure backgrounds, and children from rough or unstable backgrounds; children who had been pampered, and children who had been neglected. Above all, we had average children from average families in average areas, of average backgrounds. Some, by their appearance, were patently gay; most would pass down the street without being noticed.[19]

Since homosexuals are widely and randomly distributed through all sections of society, there is no justification at all for the politicisation of homosexuality along party lines. The fact that they will be found amongst the supporters of all parties — and amongst their children — should discourage politicians from promoting measures expressly contrived to diminish the likelihood that youngsters coming to terms with their homosexuality will find sympathy, understanding and help. Though many may fail or refuse to recognise it, it is in the interests of all to encourage acceptance and toleration rather than bigotry and prejudice.

How large a proportion of the population is homosexual? In the 1960's the generally accepted estimate was one in twenty. A book on the subject even took this ratio as its title.[20] Some gay activists now propagate figures which are much higher. According to some estimates, homosexuals are proliferating more rapidly than Falstaff's men in buckram suits.[21] The London Gay Teenage Group and *Changing the World*[22] put the numbers at one in ten, and some now pretend that as many as one in five is homosexual.[23] Such wildly exaggerated and implausible claims as the last one do nothing to further the interests of homosexual equality. On the other hand, Tingle maintains that the number is more like one in twenty—five for men and one in forty—five for women.[24] Her motive for wishing to understate the extent of homosexuality is presumably that the phenomenon could more easily be ignored if its incidence were very small. However, even if the percentage were as low as she would like to believe, it would still represent a very large number of people in absolute terms. Moreover, even if homosexuals constituted only one person in a hundred, it would not for that reason be equitable to maltreat them. The agencies which specialise in helping homosexuals as well as those with wider aims such as the Samaritans know only too well that young homosexuals are badly treated, even when the only problems they have to contend with are the onerous psychological pressures of concealment, pretence, and fear of parental rejection. In the next chapter I shall suggest how their lot might be improved by promoting through the educational system more widespread understanding of the nature and extent of homosexuality.

5. Gay Lessons: Homosexuality and the Curriculum.

In the first chapter I established that homosexuality is not unnatural, and in the second I argued that it is not wrong. In the previous chapter I described the unhappiness and suffering — sometimes intense — which are caused to young homosexuals as they grow up in a world which views their sexuality as alien and treats them with hostility. Given that a significant proportion of young people *will* grow up to be homosexual, the education provided by our schools should seek both to equip them to live their lives to good effect and to instil in others a conscionable degree of understanding and acceptance of them. As Ealing's policy statement points out:

> It is vital that they are reassured that homosexuality is not a disease or "perversion" but simply another variation of human sexuality. Many pupils will also be unsure as to their sexuality, and it is important that they are able to decide for themselves without being subjected to pressure at school. Education also involves encouraging respect for and acceptance of others. In the course of their lives, children may have friends, relatives, or their own daughters and sons who form lesbian or gay relationships. This is why we need to overcome prejudice against homosexuality... we...wish to create an educational atmosphere in which all pupils are able to recognise, with confidence, their developing sexuality. It is also important to dispel

42

the myths built up by the negative and often derogatory images of lesbians and gay men shown in society. [1]

This policy identifies two objectives: (1) to reassure those who grow up to be homosexual that they are not therefore ill or wicked but rather that their sexuality is a perfectly common and healthy phenomenon about which they need have no regrets; (2) to promote in those who do not grow up to be homosexual an understanding of what homosexuality is so that they will accept workmates, friends, and perhaps even their own children who might be.

The opponents of the positive treatment of homosexuality, aided and abetted by shallow, irresponsible, and dishonest coverage by the tabloid press, have deployed a number of arguments to justify their stance. Some of these (e.g. that it is unnatural, that it is a mental illness, that it is inherently wicked, and that it is socially subversive) I have dealt with in earlier chapters. However, there are a couple of other arguments which need to be addressed. One is that the real aim of those who advocate 'gay lessons' is to convert young people to homosexuality. As I admitted in Chapter 1, some material emanating from unrepresentative sources *does* give the impression that sexual orientation is a matter of choice. A few extremely radical feminists appear to have renounced heterosexuality in favour of lesbianism as a matter of principle. There may also be some evenly balanced bisexuals to whom such a choice is open; but most people are strongly predisposed in one direction or the other and would not be susceptible to 'sexual conversion' of the kind envisaged. Fears about the proselytising aims of 'positive image' policies may well have been aggravated by a failure to note the distinction between *heterosexuality* and *heterosexism*. Opposition to heterosexism implies antipathy not to heterosexuality but rather to the view that the only legitimate sexual relationships are heterosexual. Thus when people strive to combat heterosexism they are seeking only to promote a climate in which homosexual relationships can be accepted on the same terms as heterosexual ones.

A recent contributor to the *Times Educational Supplement* evidently thinks that most young people's heterosexuality is so precarious that the mere mention of homosexuality will send them rushing from the classroom to conduct lurid and lascivious experiments. [2] Those who are keen to emphasise the possibility of proselytisation tend to espouse the view that homosexuality is the result of immaturity or corruption; that inside every homosexual is a budding heterosexual who is trying to break out and whose chances of doing so are enhanced by the application of appropriate psychological and social pressures. Since it would undermine such influences, they are steadfastly opposed to anything which might promote more widespread understanding of homosexuality. This attitude is both unscientific and unjust. If proselytisation *were* a possibility, their objections might have some validity, for they would be justified in wanting to protect their children from unwarrantable interference with their autonomy. However, all the real force of this argument in on the other side; for, as we have seen in the previous chapter, those who grow up to be homosexual face pressures which are always to some extent baneful and are often so great that they prove insupportable. The question which parents and politicians need to ask themselves is whether they would want a child of their own who grew up to be homosexual to be subject to abuse and vilification or perhaps driven to such profound despair that he attempted suicide. Since prospective parents and those whose children are still young can by no means be certain that their offspring will be heterosexual, they must make their choice of educational policy from behind a Rawlsian 'veil of ignorance'. [3]

While there is no evidence that the positive

44

treatment of homosexuality will undermine anyone's capacity to be heterosexual, it is certain that failure to deal constructively with it will inhibit the potential of many young people to be happy. In the past, images of homosexuals projected by the entertainment media were almost invariably stereotypes contrived to evoke either ridicule or contempt. More recently, however, there have been at least some sympathetic depictions of non−stereotyped homosexual characters. [4] As was mentioned in Chapter 3, news coverage, quite naturally, tends to concentrate on the salacious and seamy. This is equally true of heterosexuality: for adultery or other sexual indiscretions − particularly if they involve the famous − are newsworthy in a way in which the ordinary course of domestic life is not. However, while such aspects of heterosexuality, being constantly outweighed by direct experience of relatively stable family life, will be seen for the aberrations which they are, the same is not true of negative portrayals of homosexuality, which are likely to be accepted as genuinely representative even by gay people themselves − especially while they are still young and have no contrary experience to redress the demeaning images which assail them. Adam Mars−Jones has recently made this point to particularly good effect.

> Gay people have none of the benefits of being brought up by fellow−members of their minority. Members of other minorities may have unpleasant lessons to learn, but at least Jewish children learn about Hanukkah before holocaust, Passover before pogrom... Homosexuals...are poorly placed to rebut even the most preposterous description of homosexuality. *This isn't true of me*, many gay people may think, *but perhaps it is true of the majority of my minority. How can I know?...* When a book called *Queens*...appeared a few years ago, Gay Switchboard received a number of distress calls from people who wanted to know if the book was accurate, in which case they proposed

to end it all. Is there another minority that genuinely wouldn't know the difference between an accurate portrait and a piece of sensationalist fantasy? [5]

There is also the danger that negative portrayals of homosexuals can be self — fulfilling; for when young homosexuals lack positive images on which to model themselves they are more likely to become all the bad things which they are made out to be. Accordingly, since homosexuality is more shrouded in ignorance than heterosexuality, there is — if anything — an even greater need to give it a place in the curriculum.

Another objection implied by Tingle is that homosexuality is likely to be dealt with in an amoral way, "with emphasis on individual gratification rather than an interpersonal act". [6] There is no reason why this *need* be so, and many reasons why it should not be. She refers to books produced in the 1970's which appear to countenance behaviour of a purely self — indulgent, gratificatory kind. [7] I suspect that she does not know to what extent such material is used, and I do not pretend to. Inasmuch as any programme of sex education did commend transient, impersonal, and exploitative sexual encounters I should strongly disapprove of it, and am confident that most parents would share my disapprobation. However in advancing this objection, Tingle is being disingenuous. For she and the lobby which she represents condemn not just degenerate manifestations of homosexuality but homosexuality *tout court*, and therefore censure anything which might induce greater self — respect in homosexuals or promote more accommodating attitudes in others towards them.

Now Ealing's policy expressly requires that homosexuality, like heterosexuality, should be discussed in the context of love, personal relationships, home life, and respect for others and is therefore invulnerable to the imputation of amoralism, but this has not secured it against malicious calumnies.[8]   Indeed, although it is a model of reasonableness and moderation, it has been the object of unwavering hostility from the all too numerous intellectual descendants of Lady Bracknell, who, it will be remembered, disapproved of anything which tampers with natural ignorance.[9]   When Tingle says that she is not against the objective treatment of homosexuality[10], she means that it should be projected as an illness or a perversion.   Elsewhere her disapproval of attempts to eradicate homophobia is made unashamedly manifest.[11] In view of Tingle's apprehensions about amoralistic treatment of sexuality, the recent legislation is particularly ironic, since, while expressly permitting the mention of homosexuality as a possible harbinger of a fatal disease, it prohibits the presentation in state schools of even the most stable homosexual cohabitation as 'a pretended family relationship' or the suggestion that such a lifestyle is 'acceptable'.[12]   It therefore strikes right at the heart of a policy such as Ealing's or of proposals such as my own, which aim explicitly to put homosexuality into the emotional and moral context of caring relationships.

The results of a survey published in the *Times Educational Supplement* of 7th November 1986 indicate that an overwhelming majority (87%) of teachers believe that sex education should emphasise traditional values and be taught in the context of family life — a view from which only 6% dissented.   It is therefore fairly certain that most of the third (34%) who expressed the view that homosexuality should be presented as an acceptable way of living would favour stable rather than casual relationships.   It is disconcerting that almost exactly the same proportion of teachers should think that homosexuality is *not* an acceptable way of living.   24% thought that it should be so presented, and one must conclude that the 11% who said that the subject should not be covered at all have censorious attitudes.   It is rather surprising that 31% expressed no opinion in this matter.   The same page of the TES carried details of a survey commissioned by the television programme *This*

Week of 500 viewers, 76% of whom wanted homosexuality to be treated as deviant behaviour or not mentioned at all. I am far from thinking that such bigotry should be acquiesced in. It rather indicates how great is the need to disseminate accurate information, by which it may be dispelled.

Understanding of homosexuality might well be effectively promoted if more homosexual teachers were willing to 'come out' at school. However, this is a classic case of the vicious circle: if more homosexual teachers were out, there would be more understanding and acceptance: if there were more understanding and acceptance, then more gay teachers would feel able to come out. Setting aside irrational fears, there are no *a priori* reasons why homosexuals should not be teachers. Speaking in the House of Commons in December 1987, Mr. Ken Livingstone observed that in his thirteen years as a member of the Inner London Education Authority, every known instance of sexual abuse was of a heterosexual male teacher assaulting girls. [13] Contrary then to popular myth, there is no great probability that a homosexual teacher will be a corruptive influence. Writing on this very issue over twenty years ago in his *Ethics and Education*, a work which quickly established itself as a classic, R.S. Peters remarked:

> ...a teacher may join some society in his spare time for the amelioration of the condition of homosexuals in society. Parents and indignant citizens might band together and start an agitation to have him dismissed from his post, as a source of corruption... What would have to be produced, however, would be concrete evidence of corruption or incompetence. General probabilities are not enough. If this demand were once abandoned the teacher's position in the community would become intolerable. [14]

The ethos of a school (sometimes called 'the hidden curriculum') is clearly important in combatting prejudice. Anti–homosexual abuse and distasteful jokes should always be challenged and their perpetrators reprimanded. However, one cannot expect such a policy to be any more successful than more orthodox didactic enterprises. As Andrew Stark has pointed out[15], most anti–gay behaviour comes from the children of parents who themselves profess bigoted attitudes. This accords with a general observation made in 1723 by Bernard Mandeville, who was sceptical of the capacity of institutional education to bring about moral improvement.

> It is Precept and the Example of Parents, and those they Eat, Drink, and Converse with, that have an Influence upon the Minds of Children: Reprobate Parents that take ill Courses...won't have a mannerly civiliz'd Offspring though they went to....school till they were married.[16]

Although the best endeavours may meet with little success, the task of trying to eradicate prejudice should not be abandoned.

Even if there were no legal impediments to dealing constructively in schools with homosexuality, and every local education authority were warmly disposed to such a project, there is a great dearth of material suitable for use in the classroom. This is hardly surprising: for who would produce a commodity for which there is no market? In September 1986, the Inner London Education Authority published a *Materiography* of what is available.[17] While this was an honest and enterprising attempt to meet a real need, my selective reading prompts me to suspect that much of what it contains is unsuitable for use in schools, though it may be more appropriate for colleges. Firstly, many of the books are American and therefore contain words and allusions which will be unfamiliar to English pupils. Secondly, they are written for an older readership and would have no direct appeal to adolescents. Thirdly, although some of the books are highly competent, others are execrably written trash.

I should unhesitatingly place David Rees's *The Milkman's on his Way* in the former category, but it was not written as a school text book, and its explicit descriptions of sexual activity, while constituting less than 1% of its linage, would disqualify it for this purpose. Also, in view of the possibility of contracting AIDS from certain kinds of sexual activity — greatly increased as it is since Rees's book first appeared — it might be argued that its sexually explicit passages should be amended so as to recommend precautions against the transmission of this disease. Moreover, one must face squarely up to the question as to whether all its characters deserve to count as positive ones. As I make clear in the previous chapter, Ewan, the hero of the book, is more sinned against than sinning and manages to surmount the obstacles which confront many young gay people. However, it includes prominent elements which make it a 'warts and all' portrait of gay life. The 23 year−old teacher who seduces Ewan realises that he is sexually frustrated and starved of affection and therefore extremely impressionable and vulnerable, but this does not deter him from his wanton plan of seduction, after which he strings him along for a week, and then abandons him without even a phone number or address through which contact can be maintained. Since he evidently has no real concern for Ewan, his conduct seems to me profoundly reprehensible, and certainly no example worthy of imitation. Rees also includes descriptions of gay venues and of the effects of promiscuity. To his credit, these are by no means alluring.

The gay clubs: their ridiculous names, ·suggestive of all sorts of heaven on earth, their cheap glitter and high prices, their lights subtle enough to deceive everyone into thinking everyone else was good−looking..., the crowds of lonely men waiting for Mr. Right to walk through the door, eyeing every newcomer and only seeing Mr. Compromise, the pick−ups, the rejections, the certainty for most of only a one−night stand at best...[18]

...the procedure, when it's possible to have sex with almost anyone, was for me becoming sterile and meaningless, not even physically very exciting.[19]

So honest an account hardly constitutes an inducement to promiscuity. At the same time, it does not provide a clear model of anything better.

One book which can be unreservedly recommended is Timothy Ireland's short novel *Who lies inside* − an extremely unpretentious little book which is yet permeated by the most humane ideals and the most responsible moral values. It tells how Martin Conway, an eighteen−year−old who is about to leave school and go to a college of education, comes to realise and to accept his homosexuality despite adverse pressure from his contemporaries and his fears of parental disapproval. He is attracted to one of his classmates, Richard, who appears to give him encouraging signs of reciprocity; but Martin is inhibited from developing this relationship, and in compliance with the expressed wishes of his other friends starts dating a girl called Margaret, with whom before long he has sexual intercourse. This experience is predictably unsatisfying, and is immediately viewed with revulsion and remorse − a perception which the reader is strongly induced to share. Even before this event, his aversion to the course of action on which he has embarked is made clear.

I thought of the number of times I'd heard men boasting about how many girls they'd laid. I'd never heard any man bragging about being in love. Whilst my sexual success with Margaret, despite her hurt, would be admired, my love for Richard would be derided. It made me wonder bitterly just who was perverted, those that used others for sexual gain, or those that genuinely loved. [20]

The book incorporates many valuable lessons, both by commending the virtues of self—awareness, tolerance and respect for the feelings of others, and by depicting the misery and distress which are caused when, in violation of these principles, homosexual pegs are forced into heterosexual holes. Fortunately, Martin Conway is perceptive and strong—minded enough to retrieve himself before any further harm is done. He does not want to live a lie or to hurt anyone, but only to be able to associate freely and unashamedly with the person he truly cares for; as in fact he does in the final chapter of the book.

Since Roger Scruton is one of the five signatories to the radical manifesto *Whose Schools?*, we must suppose that he endorses its implied deprecation of 'gay lessons'[21]. I think we can also suppose that he did not trouble to inquire very carefully into what he was so ready to condemn, in which case he should perhaps be urged to take to heart six wise words of Chairman Mao: "No investigation, no right to speak"[22]. I certainly think that if he had read Timothy Ireland's novel, he might have thought twice before declaring himself an opponent of such studies; for the ideals enshrined in this book accord so well with the canons of sexual propriety enjoined in his own voluminous tome *Sexual Desire*. In fact, I could hardly imagine a work of modern fiction which promoted them more eloquently. The attachment between Martin and Richard has all the makings of an ideal *Scrutonian relationship*. (I coin this term to mean 'a caring and committed erotic relationship founded on reciprocal sexual desire with full interpersonal intentionality'.) Although Scruton is less than happy about such relationships between persons of the same sex, there is nothing in his book which shows them to be impossible, and much to suggest the contrary.

Accordingly, if he really believes all that he has written, he must surely prefer a Scrutonian relationship between two persons of the same sex to a heterosexual relationship which lacks intentionality and is therefore, in his view, 'perverted'[23]. Thus Roger Scruton, Martin Conway, and (presumably) the author who created him are unanimous on this point: whether they be gay or straight, it is those that use others without loving them, not those who genuinely love, who are perverted.

In a recent article[24] I pointed out that if Roger Scruton is consistent, he is bound to endorse the positive treatment of homosexuality by moral educators. The penultimate chapter of his book *Sexual Desire* is concerned with the scope and purpose of sexual morality and the objectives of moral education in matters sexual. I am entirely sympathetic to his recommendations, which are supported by the arguments I have deployed in Chapter 2. He advocates that moral education should guide us towards a state in which our sexuality is entirely integrated into the life of personal affection, and in which the self and its responsibility are centrally involved and indissolubly linked to the pleasures and passions of the body.[25]

This recommendation, which I am delighted to endorse, has corollaries which Scruton must surely find alarmingly radical. As he himself admits, "sexual desire does not occur only between people of different sex; any account of sexual desire that could not be extended to homosexuality would be ludicrous."[26] By the same token, any ideology of sexuality or programme of moral education which ignores the needs of so large a minority must be accounted inadequate. Since many young people will turn out to be so orientated, should not wise and benevolent educators, unfettered by superstition and prejudice, take all practicable care to supply their needs? On Scruton's own admission, homosexual desire is capable of the same interpersonal intentionality as heterosexual desire, and homosexual relationships therefore have precisely the same potential. However, homosexuals can hardly be prepared for erotic love and encouraged towards a lifestyle in which their sexuality is "entirely integrated into the life of personal affection" if, as has traditionally been the case, they are constantly admonished to depreciate themselves and their sexual nature and offered no support by social norms and institutions.

Homosexuality must therefore be actively recognised and constructively dealt with by moral educators. They must provide reassurance that it is a common, natural and healthy condition and that it is no less possible for homosexuals than for heterosexuals to have happy and fulfilling relationships. They must present positive role models of well—adjusted and responsible homosexuals which those who grow up to be gay can identify with and imitate, and which those who do not can respect and admire. All those who continue to obstruct such proposals must bear a heavy responsibility for the evils which will continue to flow from the problems they have so wilfully ignored — problems which were examined in Chapter 4. Writing of a sample of over four hundred used in a survey commissioned by the London Gay Teenage Group, the researchers point out:

Over half had been verbally abused, a fifth had been beaten up, one in ten had been thrown out of home and many others sent to a doctor or psychiatrist because they were lesbian or gay. One in five had felt under such intolerable pressure that they had attempted suicide. It is indicative of the strength of these young people that they have all survived these crises and are now happy to identify themselves to us as homosexual.

[They] have exhibited a strength in coping with society's prejudices, and have celebrated their sexuality in a way that other generations should envy. At 20 or under they have identified themselves positively as lesbian or gay, have formed relationships, made friends and established lifestyles. On the other hand, we have also read or heard about ways in which homosexuals are discriminated against, the prejudice, ignorance and bigotry which they experience. We have read or heard how those close to them, and society in general, have shunned, rejected, or abused them because they are homosexual. [27]

Those who are so obdurate and callous as to feel no sympathy towards this needless suffering should reflect that they or their friends or relations may well have homosexual children who are similarly at risk. The issues I have discussed desperately require more candid and dispassionate treatment that they have recently received. Let us hope that fair dealing and honest inquiry will soon overcome the insolent bigotry which now exults in its recent triumph.

Notes and References.

1. **Is Homosexuality Natural?**

1. HUME, David *A Treatise of Human Nature,* revised by P.H. Nidditch (Oxford: Clarendon Press, 1978) p.474. (First published in 1740.)
2. WESTERMARCK, Edward *The Origin and Development of the Moral Ideas* Vol. II (London: Macmillan, 1917) p.456.
3. WEEKS, Jeffrey *Coming Out — Homosexual Politics in Britain, from the Nineteenth Century to the Present* (London: Quartet Books, 1977) p.3.
4. Ibid. p.12.
5. Ibid. p.27.
6. ROGERS, Adrian and CLEMENTS, Bill *The Moral Basis of Freedom* (Exeter: Victoria Books, 1985) p.37.
7. TINGLE, Rachel *Gay Lessons — How Public Funds are used to promote Homosexuality among Children and Young People* (London: Pickwick Books, 1986) p.2.
8. LOCKE, John *An Essay concerning Human Understanding*, edited by P.H.Nidditch (Oxford: Clarendon Press, 1975) p.657. (First published in 1690.)
9. BURBAGE, Michael and WALTERS, Jonathan (Editors) *Breaking the Silence — Gay Teenagers speak for themselves.* (London: Joint Council for Gay Teenagers, 1981). See also Chapter 4.
10. HUTCHESON, Francis *An Inquiry into the Original of our Ideas of Beauty and Virtue,* Fourth Edition (London, 1738) pp. xi—xii.

11. See for example *Changing the World — a London Charter for Gay and Lesbian Rights* p.8, where it says: "...how can we say that only 10% of the population is lesbian or gay when many of us never consider we have a choice of sexuality as that 'choice' is so clearly an unequal one. Heterosexuality is energetically encouraged..." Similarly in the Appendix to Hugh Warren's *Talking about School* (London Gay Teenage Group, 1984) it is claimed that "sexuality can be a matter of active and positive choice". (p.48)

12. HOLBROOK, David *Sex and Dehumanization* (London: Pitman, 1972) pp.94–111. The sample here cited is of twelve psychiatric patients.

13. WHITEHOUSE, Mary *Whatever happened to Sex?* (Hove: Wayland Publishers, 1977) pp.66–8. Whitehouse quotes a self–denigrating remark made by Quentin Crisp ("I am only half a person"), refers to a report published as long ago as 1951, and another of 1955 which documents the release from homosexual tendencies of fourteen patients who underwent 'spiritual conversion'.

14. TINGLE, op. cit. p.3.

15. BROAD, Charles Dunbar *Critical Essays in Moral Philosophy*, edited by David Cheney (London: Allen & Unwin, 1971) p.169.

16. FLEW, Antony Letter in the *Bulletin of the Campaign for Homosexual Equality*, May, 1971.

17. LAYLAND, Joyce 'What everybody knows' *Manchester Parents' Group Newsletter* Summer, 1987.

18. See BAILEY, D. Sherwin *Homosexuality and the Western Church Tradition* (London: Longman, Green & Co., 1955) and BOSWELL, John *Christianity, Social Tolerance and Homosexuality* (University of Chicago Press, 1980).

19. *Letter to the Bishops of the Catholic Church on the Pastoral Care of Homosexual Persons* (London: Catholic Truth Society, 1986) p.3.

20. Ibid. pp.4 & 8.

21. *Leviticus* 18:22 and 20:13, *Romans* 1: 18−32, *1 Corinthians* 6:9.
22. *Heart of the Matter*, BBC 1, 6th September, 1987.
23. Op. cit. pp. 8−9.
24. BEATTIE, James *An Essay on the Nature and Immutability of Truth...* Sixth Edition (London: Edward & Charles Dilly, 1778) p.201. Cardinal Ratzinger, whose name I have substituted for that of Malebranche, is the first signatory of the Pastoral Letter.

2. Is Homosexuality Wrong?

1. ROGERS and CLEMENTS, op. cit. p.36.
2. See Chapter 3.
3. See my 'Hutcheson, Hume and the Ontology of Morals' *Journal of Value Inquiry* Vol. 19 No. 2 (1985) pp.133−151.
4. HUME, D. op. cit. p.469.
5. See my 'Hume, Spencer and the Standard of Morals' *Philosophy* Vol. 58 (1983) pp.39−55, especially Section I, pp. 40−48.
6. SPENCER, Herbert *First Principles*, Fifth Edition, (London: Williams & Norgate, 1893) p.360.
7. SPENCER, Herbert *The Principles of Ethics*, 2 vols. (London: Williams & Norgate, 1897−1900) Vol. I p.466.
8. See my 'Hume, Spencer and the Standard of Morals' (note 5 above) Section II, pp. 48−52.
9. I first propounded this thesis in 'On Distinguishing between Love and Lust' *Journal of Value Inquiry* Vol. 11 No.4 (1977). More recently, in his book *Sexual Desire* (see 10 below) Roger Scruton has claimed that human sexuality is *essentially* intentional (pp.29−36) − a view which I have criticised at length in Section I of my discussion article 'Love and Lust Revisited: Intentionality, Homosexuality, and Moral Education' *Journal of Applied Philosophy* Vol. 1 No. 5 (1988) pp.89−102.

58

10. SCRUTON, Roger *Sexual Desire* (London: Weidenfeld & Nicolson, 1986) p.305.
11. ROGERS and CLEMENTS op. cit. p.18.
12. Ibid. p.22.
13. Some people have argued that the term *promiscuity* is meangingless because it is impossible to pronounce definitively of some behaviour whether it is promiscuous or not. I find this objection unconvincing. There are most certainly modes of conduct which are paradigmatically promiscuous (e.g. that of people who deliberately avail themselves of innumerable casual encounters). There is also conduct which is paradigmatically *not* promiscuous (e.g. that of a person who lives faithfully for a lifetime or for many years with one partner). More problematic is the situation of someone who in the quest for a stable relationship embarks on a number of liaisons which prove abortive. How many frogs should he expect to go to bed with before meeting the one who turns into a handsome prince/beautiful princess? In his book *Sexual Morality* (London: Hutchinson, 1965) Ronald Atkinson used the term *promiscuity* to encompass "less durable...liaisons...in which there is...the intention to keep deep emotional involvement and personal commitment to a minimum" (p.74). By this definition, which I find attractive, the criterion is related more to intention than to conduct.
14. SPENCER, H. *The Principles of Ethics* (see note 7 above) Vol. 1 p.463.
15. SPENCER, H. *Education: Intellectual, Moral and Physical* (London: G. Manwaring, 1861 — subsequent editions, Williams & Norgate) p.60.
16. SCRUTON, R. op. cit., especially Chapter 11.

3. The Legacy of Liberationism.

1. WEEKS, Jeffrey *Coming Out — Homosexual Politics in Britain, from the Nineteenth Century to*

the Present. (London: Quartet Books, 1977) p.186.

2. WATNEY, Simon 'The Ideology of GLF' in *Homosexuality: Power and Politics* edited by Gay Left Collective (London: Allison & Busby, 1980) pp.64−7.

3. WEEKS Op. cit. p.202.

4. GREEN, Stephen 'The Abolition of the Family' in *Family Matters* (Journal of the Conservative Family Campaign) Vol. 1 No. 2 (1986). See also Tingle op. cit. pp.5−6. Rogers and Clements do not adduce any evidence in support of their claim that "homosexuality is fundamentally anti−family and anti−society" (op. cit. p.36), but pronouncements of the type in the GLF manifesto could have been cited to make their fears seem more plausible.

5. *Bulletin of the Campaign for Homosexual Equality*, November 1971.

6. 'Child−lovers win fight for role in Gay Lib' *The Guardian*, 26th August, 1975.

7. 'London Letter' *The Guardian*, 28th August, 1975.

8. 'London Letter' *The Guardian*, 10th September, 1975.

9. WHITEHOUSE, Mary *A Most Dangerous Woman?* (Tring: Lion Publishing, 1982) pp. 160−170.

10. An exception is furnished by the Lesbian and Gay Christian Movement, who in a document prepared in October 1987 for the forthcoming Church of England Synod *(Briefing No. 1)* admitted quite candidly that AIDS is spread by sexual promiscuity.

4. Where Ignorance isn't Bliss.

1. TINGLE, Rachel *Gay Lessons* (See Chapter 1, Note 7) pp.21 and 42.

2. Ibid. pp. iii, 21 and 42. Also in the article in *The Free Nation* (see Chapter 5, Note 8).

3. Ibid. p.42.

4. REES, David *The Milkman's on his Way* (London: Gay Men's Press, 1982) pp.14−5.

5.   Ibid. p.60.
6.   Ibid. p.37.
7.   In the most extreme case to come to my notice, a man evicted his thirteen−year−old son on being told that he was gay. Although the boy went missing for nine weeks, his parents did not report his absence to the police or take steps to locate him.
8.   Ibid. p.70.
9.   Ibid. p.61.
10. Ibid. p.63.
11. Ibid. p.65.
12. See Chapter 1, Note 9.
13. TRENCHARD, Lorraine and WARREN, Hugh *Something to tell you* (London: London Gay Teenage Group, 1984).
14. Ibid. p.132.
15. HALL, Catherine 'Young Homosexuals − How we fail them' *Times Educational Supplement* 15th January, 1988.
16. STARK, Andrew 'Gays and the Pastoral System' in *School's Out*, second edition, (London: Gay Teachers' Group, 1987) pp.43−4.
17. See Chapter 5, Note 2.
18. *Something to tell you* (see 13 above) p.28.
19. ROBERTSON, Rose 'My Son the Football' *Open Mind* (Journal of the Conservative Group for Homosexual Equality) No.3 (1987).
20. MAGEE, Brian *One in Twenty* (London: Secker & Warburg, 1966).
21. SHAKESPEARE, William *King Henry IV, Part I* Act II, Scene 4.
22. See Chapter 1, Note 11.
23. *The Guardian* 15th December, 1987 reported that protesters lobbying Parliament carried posters, some of which read (ungrammatically): "One in five mothers are lesbians."
24. TINGLE op. cit. p.5.

5. Gay Lessons: Homosexuality and the Curriculum.

1. London Borough of Ealing: Education Committee Policy Statement on Sexual Equality (approved on 20th January, 1987).
2. MULLEN, Peter 'Licenced to Pervert' *Times Educational Supplement,* 16th October, 1987. This article incorporates the contradictory suggestions: (i) that homosexual acts are so disgusting that only perverts would engage in them; (ii) they are so alluring that heterosexual youngsters will be 'converted' to them.
3. In his book *A Theory of Justice* (Oxford: Clarendon Press, 1972) John Rawls advocates that social arrangements should be determined as if by idealised prospective participants, who, though they possess comprehensive knowledge about psychology, sociology, economics, etc., know nothing about themselves or their own circumstances in the society they are about to join. In this respect they are therefore behind a 'veil of ignorance' (pp.136−142). Though Rawls's proposals are in general too obviously counterfactual to be seriously entertained outside of seminar rooms, homosexuality, occurring randomly as it does, provides a concrete instance to which they might arguably be applicable.
4. Several television 'soap operas' have included gay characters, and I have personally seen two excellent T.V. movies which dealt most ably with the problems faced by gay teenagers, *viz. Consenting Adult* directed by Gilbert Cates (1984 − Channel 4, 28th October, 1986) and *Welcome Home, Bobby* directed by Herbert Wise (1986 − BBC 2, 30th June, 1987).
5. MARS−JONES, Adam 'Homosexual Men as Soft Targets' *The Spectator*, 15th August, 1987.
6. TINGLE op. cit. p.14
7. The books cited by Tingle are: HILL, Maurice and LLOYD−JONES, Michael: *The Erroneous Zone* (London: National Secular Society, 1971) and

62

COUSINS, Jane: *Make it Happy* (London: Virago, 1978).

8. TINGLE, Rachel 'Gay Lessons in Haringey: Tip of Labour Iceberg' *The Free Nation* February, 1987. Tingle also castigates Ealing's policy of endorsing "respect for and acceptance of individuals and their caring relationships (including homosexual relationships)". On *The Education Programme*, BBC 2, 27th November, 1987 Baroness Cox cast aspersions upon this same policy.

9. WILDE, Oscar *The Importance of being Earnest*, Act I (1895).

10. See Tingle's reply to a letter from Professor Peter Campbell in *The Free Nation* August, 1987.

11. TINGLE, *Gay Lessons* p.vii.

12. Local Government Act (1988) Clause 28 (originally numbered 27 and briefly renumbered 29).

13. *Hansard* (Tuesday, 15th December, 1987) Vol. 124 No. 65 Column 1012. Reported in *The Daily Telegraph*, 16th December, 1987.

14. PETERS, R.S. *Ethics and Education* (London: Allen & Unwin, 1966) pp.203−4.

15. STARK, Andrew 'Gays and the Pastoral System' in *School's Out* (London: Gay Teachers' Group, 1987) p.49.

16. MANDEVILLE, Bernard *The Fable of the Bees*, edited by F.B. Kaye, 2 vols. (Oxford: Clarendon Press, 1924) I p.270. 'An Essay on...Charity Schools', from which the quotation comes, was first printed in the second edition, 1723.

17. ILEA LEARNING RESOURCES BRANCH *Positive Images* Materiography Series No. 11 (1986).

18. REES, David *The Milkman's on his Way* (London: Gay Men's Press, 1982) p.99.

19. Ibid. p.106.

20. IRELAND, Timothy *Who lies inside* (London: Gay Men's Press, 1984) p.94.

21. COX, Caroline *et al. Whose Schools?* (London: the Hillgate Group, 1986). This tract deploys emotive phrases such as "overt preaching on behalf of

homosexuality", which is glibly conjoined with "sexual licence and social indiscipline" (p.4).

22. MAO TSE−TUNG *Quotations from Chairman Mao* (Peking: Foreign Languages Press, 1966) p.230.

23. SCRUTON, Roger *Sexual Desire* (London: Weidenfeld & Nicolson, 1986) pp.289−290.

24. STAFFORD, J. Martin 'Love and Lust Revisited: Intentionality, Homosexuality, and Moral Education' *Journal of Applied Philosophy* Vol.5 No.1 (1988), Section III.

25. SCRUTON op. cit. p.346.

26. Ibid. p.254.

27. TRENCHARD, Lorraine and WARREN, Hugh *Something to tell you* (London: London Gay Teenage Group, 1984) pp.151 and 156.